W9-AVH-044

CHANGING TIMES
ANCIENT GREECE

Crime and Punishment

By Richard Dargie

Illustrated by Adam Hook

First published in 2007 by
Compass Point Books
3109 West 50th Street, #115
Minneapolis, MN 55410
Visit Compass Point Books on the Internet at www.compasspointbooks.com
or e-mail your request to custserv@compasspointbooks.com

Library of Congress Cataloging-in-Publication Data
Dargie, Richard.
  Ancient Greece, crime and punishment / by Richard Dargie ; illustrations
by Adam Hook.
     p. cm. -- (Changing times (Minneapolis, Minn.))
  Includes bibliographical references and index.
  ISBN-13: 978-0-7565-2084-7 (library binding)
  ISBN-10: 0-7565-2084-3 (library binding)
1. Crime--Greece--History--To 1500--Juvenile literature. 2. Criminals-
-Greece--History--To 1500--Juvenile literature. 3. Criminal justice,
Administration of--Greece--History--To 1500--Juvenile literature. I.
Hook, Adam. II. Title. III. Series.

HV7075.5.D37 2006
  364.938--dc22   2006027037

Picture Acknowledgments
The publishers would like to thank the following for permission to
reproduce their pictures:
AKG: 14 (John Hios), 24 (Peter Connolly). Art Archive: 6 (Archaeological
Museum, Ferrara/Dagli Orti [A]), 9 (Agora Museum, Athens/Dagli
Orti), 10 (Archaeological Museum, Florence/Dagli Orti), 13 (Jan Vinchon
Numismatist, Paris/Dagli Orti), 16 (Museo Naval, Madrid/Dagli Orti),
21 (Musée du Louvre, Paris/Dagli Orti), 22 (Dagli Orti), 26 (Dagli Orti),
28 (Agora Museum, Athens/Dagli Orti). Bridgeman Art Library: 18
(Ashmolean Museum, Oxford).

Copyright © 2007 Bailey Publishing Associates Ltd.
All rights reserved. No part of this book may be reproduced without
written permission from the publisher. The publisher takes no
responsibility for the use of any of the materials or methods described in
this book, nor for the products thereof.
Printed in the United States of America.

Contents

Introduction

Who Were the Ancient Greeks?

The ancient Greeks were a remarkable people who helped lay the foundations of our civilization. They lived in what is now Greece, on the surrounding Mediterranean islands, and on the neighboring coast of Asia Minor.

Ancient Greek civilization began on the island of Crete in about 2000 B.C. Spreading to the mainland, it reached its height during the Classical Period (480–330 B.C.). It lost political independence in about 150 B.C. to the Roman empire but played a major role in shaping Roman life.

The ancient Greeks lived in small, independent city-states. Each one consisted of a city and its surrounding farmland. The most powerful city-states were Attica (Athens) and Laconia (Sparta), a tough soldier-state. The Athenians were rich traders whose influence extended across the Mediterranean Sea. Their city was also a center for the arts and learning. It was home to some of the finest thinkers, writers, and artists the world has ever seen. The Athenians wrote and performed the first plays and developed the idea of democratic government. It is largely because of them that we remember the ancient Greeks today.

Crime and Punishment in Ancient Greece

There were no lawyers and few judges in ancient Greece. Instead, their citizens were expected to know the laws of the city and act as their own attorney in the courts, either accusing someone else or in defense of charges made by others.

The law was different for different ranks of Greek society. Male citizens enjoyed special privileges. If they were guilty of a crime, they were usually fined rather than flogged and tortured. They could also choose to flee into exile rather than be imprisoned and executed. Slaves and common folk were less lucky. They could be imprisoned or put in the stocks, a wooden frame to lock the feet and hands.

The quotations in this book include the words of the philosophers Plato and Aristotle; the playwright Aristophanes; the poet Homer; the orators Demosthenes, Lysias, and Antiphon; the historians Herodotus, Thucydides, Plutarch, and Xenophon; and the biographer of philosophers, Diogenes Laertius. All of these help to give us a fascinating picture of crime and punishment in ancient Greece.

The First Laws

In early Greek times, most people lived in the countryside in small villages and farms. Outside the scattered towns there were few laws, few courts, and no police. Men had to be able to protect their families and their goods themselves. Many disputes were settled by threats or by force. Revenge feuds between families lasting several generations were common.

A red figure vase from 460 B.C. is evidence of a battle in ancient Greece. Every man had to be able to fight to defend his family and property.

[The two armies] were like two men quarrelling across a fence ... with yardsticks in their hands, each of them fighting for his fair share in a narrow strip.

HOMER, *THE ILIAD*

The poet Homer compared a battle between the Greeks and the Trojans to a swarm of hungry flies. Homer knew that legal disputes over land were so common that his listeners knew exactly what a fight of this kind was like. Like a battle, disputes over land and goods could be very violent and frequently ended in bloodshed.

Over time, the Greeks accepted that it was better to settle their arguments peacefully, and a system of law slowly developed. In some cities, the kings acted as judges. In others, citizens met in assemblies to listen to cases and decide on a verdict.

for his fair share in a narrow strip.

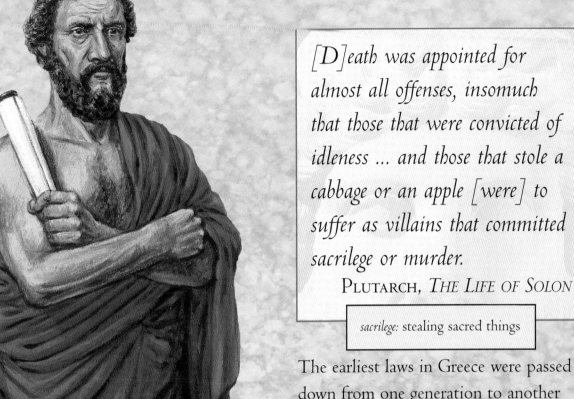

> [D]eath was appointed for almost all offenses, insomuch that those that were convicted of idleness ... and those that stole a cabbage or an apple [were] to suffer as villains that committed sacrilege or murder.
>
> PLUTARCH, *THE LIFE OF SOLON*

sacrilege: stealing sacred things

The earliest laws in Greece were passed down from one generation to another by word of mouth. The first written laws were set down by Draco of Athens in about 620 B.C. Carved onto wooden plaques and stone pillars, Draco's laws were placed in markets and other public places so that all could see and read them. As the Roman historian Plutarch shows, Draco's laws were very harsh. The Athenian orator Demades said that "Draco's laws were written in blood, not ink." Today we still call any punishment that is very harsh "draconian."

Draco served as archon, or chief magistrate, of Athens and hoped that his strict laws would calm the unruly city.

Courts and Juries

By 500 B.C. the city of Athens was a democracy. Its citizens voted for their leaders and judged legal cases in the courts. All citizens over the age of 30 could serve as a juror, and each year a list of 6,000 jurors was drawn by lottery. Juries were very large, with up to 500 jurors listening to each case. Many people were needed to sit and listen to the speeches of the accusers and defendants.

Jurors in ancient Athens recorded their decision by casting a small disk into a bronze urn.

The courts have ten entrances, one for each tribe, twenty rooms, two for each tribe ... Right to sit on juries belongs to all those over thirty years old who are not in debt to the treasury or disfranchised.

ARISTOTLE,
THE ATHENIAN CONSTITUTION

tribe: group of people
disfranchised: loss of right

As this quote shows, Athenian citizens spent much of their time in the law courts. There were many different levels within the courts, which were very organized. Any male citizen could accuse someone of a crime and take him or her to court. As a result, the city courts were always very busy.

I have not a notion how we shall dine.

Speeches made in the law courts were strictly timed using a clepsydra, or water clock. Lawyers had to stop speaking when all the water in the urn had seeped out of the hole at the bottom.

Boy: But, father, if the Archon should not form a court to-day, how are we to buy our dinner? Have you some good hope to offer us?
Chorus: Alas! Alas! I have not a notion how we shall dine.
ARISTOPHANES, THE WASPS

Archon: chief magistrate

In *The Wasps*, Aristophanes tells us that many poorer citizens needed their pay as jurors to survive. The pay was low—only two obols a day (about $5 in today's money)—so educated and able men didn't want to serve as jurors. Most jurors were elderly men who took their jury pay as a form of old-age pension. Although Aristophanes wants us to laugh at the poor jurors, he was making a serious point as well. Important law cases in Athens were often decided by uneducated people who had little knowledge of the law.

Policing Athens

In most Greek cities, law and order was kept by a small force of city guards. Each year the citizens of Athens elected 11 magistrates to keep the peace throughout the city. Known as the Eleven, they ran the city prison and were also in charge of the city's small police force. The police force was called the Scythian Archers—300 publicly owned slaves. It was the duty of the Scythian Archers to execute condemned criminals and to restore order in the streets when mobs rioted.

The Scythian Archers were named after fierce northern barbarians who were skilled warriors and horsemen.

> [I]f [a citizen] sees the homicide frequenting places of worship or the market, he may arrest him and take him to gaol.
>
> DEMOSTHENES, *AGAINST ARISTOCRATES*

the homicide: the murderer
frequenting: hanging around in
gaol: jail

In this extract from a speech, the Athenian orator Demosthenes was reminding his fellow citizens that every one of them had a duty to help keep the peace. Without a large police force, all citizens had to do their part to make sure the city's laws were respected.

> [T]en City Controllers ... keep watch to prevent any scavenger from depositing ordure within a mile and a quarter of the wall; and they prevent the construction of ... overhead conduits with an overflow into the road ... and they remove for burial the bodies of persons who die on the roads.
>
> ARISTOTLE, *THE ATHENIAN CONSTITUTION*

scavenger: person who collects items discarded by others
ordure: manure or filth
overhead conduits: raised drainpipes

Agoranomoi checked the quality and weight of foodstuffs in more than 120 Greek city-states.

This city bylaw tells us about the officials whose job it was to ensure that Athens remained a pleasant place to live. Other officials, called *agoranomoi*, were in charge of the agora, or great marketplace. They checked that the meat and fish were fresh and that nothing illegal had been added to the flour on sale. Others checked that the money was not tampered with. Anyone found guilty of breaking the city bylaws could be put in the public stocks for up to five days and nights. There they were insulted and abused by passersby.

Thieves

Most cities in ancient Greece had very strict laws against theft. Citizens who were found guilty of stealing property usually had to return the stolen object and pay the owner compensation twice its value. Citizens who embezzled, or stole money from their city's funds while acting as an official, were banished from their homeland for up to ten years. The worst thieves were thought to be the *kakourgi*, who burglarized houses at night or stole purses and fine clothes from the changing rooms in public baths and gymnasiums.

Athenian records tell us that many thieves worked in the public baths despite the strict laws against this kind of crime.

> *If he stole anything ... by night, the person aggrieved might lawfully pursue and kill or wound him, or else put him into the hands of the Eleven ... Or suppose that he stole a cloak ... from the Lyceum ... for such thefts also Solon enacted the capital penalty.*
>
> DEMOSTHENES, *AGAINST TIMOCRATES*

aggrieved: having a complaint
Lyceum: indoor sports hall
enacted the capital penalty: handed down the death penalty

In this speech, the orator Demosthenes tells us that the punishments for night thieves were especially serious. Athenians believed that a thief who broke into buildings at night was more likely to attack or even murder his victims, and the harsh penalties were designed to deter such behavior. Thieves weren't held long in the city prison. They were usually flogged, then executed.

Solon enacted the capital penalty.

stole a cloak ... from the Lyceum ... for such thefts also lawfully pursue and kill or wound him,

[T]he Eleven ... punish with death people arrested as thieves and kidnappers and footpads that confess their guilt, but if they deny the charge to bring them before the Jury-court, and if they are acquitted discharge them, but if not then to execute them.

ARISTOTLE, ON THE CONSTITUTION

footpads: thieves, muggers
discharge them: let them go

Here the writer Aristotle explains the powers of the Eleven to deal with common criminals such as thieves. If thieves were caught in the act, the Eleven executed them immediately. However, if rich and important citizens were accused of theft, they had the right to go into voluntary exile, or choose to leave the country, before the case came to court. If they stayed in the city and fought the case but then lost, they, too, were executed by the Scythian Archers.

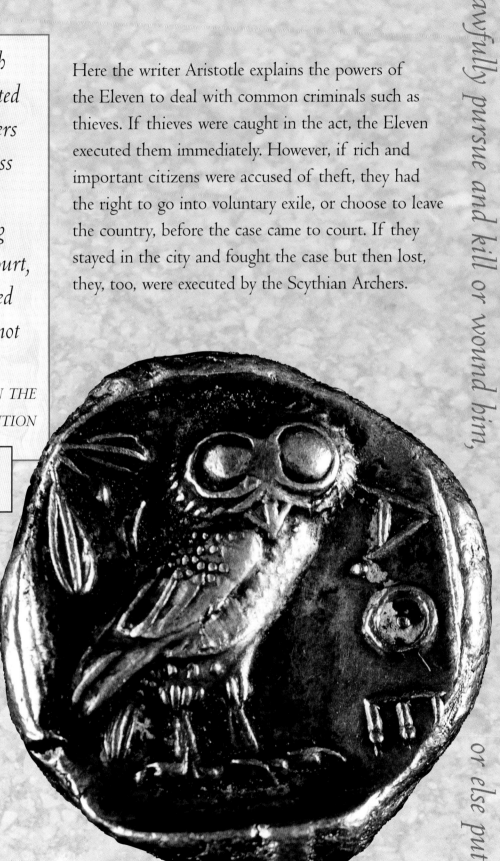

A silver tetradrachme would have been a fine prize for a fifth-century B.C. Athenian pickpocket.

If be stole anything ... by night, the person aggrieved might ... *Or suppose that he put him into the hands of the Eleven ...*

or else put

13

Murderers

In ancient Athens, murder cases were heard in the Areopagus, a special court that sat on the Ares hill above the city. This court was made up of archons, experienced judges and knowledgeable men of law. They could be trusted to give a fairer verdict than sometimes came from the large juries, which were very easily swayed by a fine speech. The archons had to make sure that the Athenian laws on murder were followed carefully.

[C]ome to the victim's aid, punish his murderer, and cleanse the city. Do this, and you will do three beneficial things: you will reduce the number of ... criminals; you will increase that of the godfearing; and you will ... be rid of the defilement which rests upon you.

ANTIPHON, *The Anonymous Prosecution for Murder*

beneficial: good
defilement: uncleanliness

Up to 300 Athenian citizens sat around the small hill in the foreground to listen to murder cases. They also listened to other serious charges such as arson, treason, and sacrilege.

In this speech, the orator Antiphon was calling on judges to make sure that murder victims were properly avenged. Severe punishments for convicted murderers encouraged others to behave well, he believed. The excerpt also tells us that the ancient Greeks believed that murder was an unclean act. Anyone such as a court juror who came into contact with a murderer had to wash himself in public afterward.

that of the godfearing; and you will ... be rid of the

> *[O]ne who was a practicer of the five games of skill, having ... unawares ... struck and killed Epitimus the Pharsalian, his father spent a whole day ... in a serious dispute, whether the javelin, or the man who threw it ... were ... to be accounted the cause of this mischance.*
>
> PLUTARCH, *LIFE OF PERICLES*

javelin: long throwing spear

This story tells us that the ancient Greeks had specific rules about what was and what was not murder. In their eyes, some killing was allowed. A householder could kill a burglar without fear of punishment afterward as long as he did so right away. If he thought about it and delayed before acting, he could be charged with murder. In the same way, citizens traveling in the countryside could legally kill a highwayman as long as they killed him immediately.

Highwaymen and bandits were common in the wild, hilly landscape of ancient Greece.

15

Pirates

Pirates were common along the coast of ancient Greece because of the many inlets where they could anchor their ships. Some pirates were soldiers who fought for rich cities such as Corinth and Athens in wartime. Others were Etruscan raiders who sailed out of their ports in Italy.

> *[A] company of sea-raiders ... were forced by bad weather to land on the Egyptian coast ... [A]n Egyptian ... hurried off ... and told Psammetichus that bronze men ... were plundering the country ... Psammetichus made friends with the raiders, and by the promise of rich rewards persuaded them to enter his service ...*
>
> HERODOTUS, *THE HISTORIES*

bronze men: men wearing bronze-colored armor
enter his service: work for him

This story, recorded by the Greek historian Herodotus, proves that many pirates were soldiers who turned to raiding to make a living in times of peace. Some pirate leaders, such as the fourth-century B.C. mercenary soldier Charidemus of Euboea, were very powerful. Charidemus built a fleet that was strong enough to capture three small towns, and Athens had to buy him off by making him a citizen.

In their fast triremes, or galleys, Greek pirates could easily raid a small town and escape before help arrived from Athens.

part of it.

placing this against the tower broke through

Pyrrhichus ... and Heracleus ... invaded our house with many other persons armed with swords and incontinently knocked down the street door, and placing this against the tower broke through part of it.

COMPLAINT BY AN ATTICA FARMER AFTER A PIRATE RAID IN 113 A.D.

incontinently: without restraint

Many Greek pirates were mercenaries who turned to piracy because they could not find work as soldiers in years of peace.

This letter was written by a farmer in Attica seeking compensation. It tells us that pirate bands attacked inland farms and that farmers built towers to try to defend their property. Pirate bands rustled (stole) the livestock and carried off people to sell to slave traders.

Greek villages often moved away from the coast and built citadels, or forts, on inland hilltops for protection. The citizens of Athens built watchtowers along the coast and at the entrance to narrow sea channels. Captured pirates were dealt with very severely. Many were chained and sent to work in the deep silver mines at Laurion, near Athens, which meant certain death.

The Powerless

In ancient Athens only citizens had full legal rights. Most inhabitants of the city had very few rights. These powerless people included women, immigrants, and slaves.

> *She [a slave girl] gave Philoneos the ... draught; ... only when the mischief was done did she see that my stepmother had tricked her ... Philoneos expired instantly; ... the subordinate who carried out the deed has been punished as she deserved, although the crime in no sense originated from her.*
>
> ANTIPHON, *PROSECUTION OF A STEPMOTHER FOR POISONING*

draught: dose of poison
mischief: bad thing
expired: died
subordinate: servant

Many slaves were prisoners taken in war, like the chained Spartans captured by the Athenians in 425 B.C.

Antiphon's story shows us that in ancient Greece, people of different social rank were treated very differently by the law. Slaves had few legal rights of their own. If a slave was assaulted or injured, justice and any compensation was owed to the slave's owner. Women and slaves were not even allowed to speak in court. Their evidence had to be presented by the master of their household. Slaves did have some rights, however. In Athens, slaves that were badly treated by their masters could take refuge in a temple called the Theseion and ask to be sold to another, kinder master.

appearance are concerned, the common people look just the

> Now, as for the slaves and
> metics in Athens, they lead a
> most undisciplined life; one is
> not permitted to strike them
> there, and a slave will not stand
> out of the way for you ...
> so far as clothing and general
> appearance are concerned, the
> common people look just the
> same as the slaves and metics.
> PSEUDO-XENOPHON,
> THE CONSTITUTION OF ATHENS

metic: a foreigner who paid a fee
to live in Athens

The author of this quote was exaggerating, but his complaint shows that although they had few legal rights, many slaves and immigrants in ancient Greece were rich. Proving that you really were a citizen was therefore very important. Several surviving law cases are about people claiming the rank of citizen. You had to be able to bring witnesses to court or bribe the jurors to prove that your claims were true.

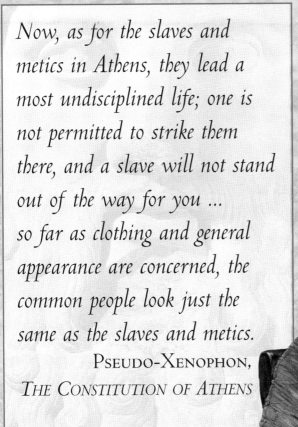

House slaves had an easier life than some in Athens, but they could still be beaten if they angered their owner.

Executing Criminals

Serious criminals such as murderers and kidnappers were put to death. In early Athens, the guilty were sometimes thrown into a pit of sharp spikes called the *barathron*. Usually only murderers suffered this sort of punishment, although women caught secretly spying on the male competitors at the Olympic Games were flung from Mount Typaeum into a deep chasm. The Spartans also cast their criminals into a disused dry well.

The barathron was a deep fissure in the rock behind the Acropolis hill in Athens.

> *Agoratus ... had three brothers. One of them ... was caught in Sicily making traitorous signals to the enemy, and by Lamachus' order he was executed on the plank. The second abducted a slave from our city to Corinth ... he was cast into prison and put to death.*
>
> LYSIAS, *AGAINST AGORATUS*

executed on the plank: crucified
abducted: kidnapped

Lysias made this speech in a court case against one of his enemies. It mentions execution on the wooden board that the Greeks called *apotumpanismos*. The guilty were chained around the neck, wrists, and ankles, then nailed to a long wooden plank. Usually they were left on the plank to die of starvation and exposure to the weather, birds, and insects. If the criminal was lucky, he died quickly, strangled by the tight iron collar around his neck.

[T]he tragic poet Antiphon, when he was about to be flogged to death by order of Dionysius, seeing that those who were to die with him covered their faces as they passed through the gates, said, "Why cover your faces? Is it because you are afraid that one of the crowd should see you tomorrow?"

ARISTOTLE, *THE ART OF RHETORIC*

Antiphon was mocking his fellow inmates who were ashamed to die by public execution in front of a large crowd. The families of the condemned were also shamed by this kind of punishment. Some Greek cities banned relatives from inheriting wealth from an executed criminal. In Athens, families were not even allowed to bury a condemned relative anywhere within the city-state of Attica.

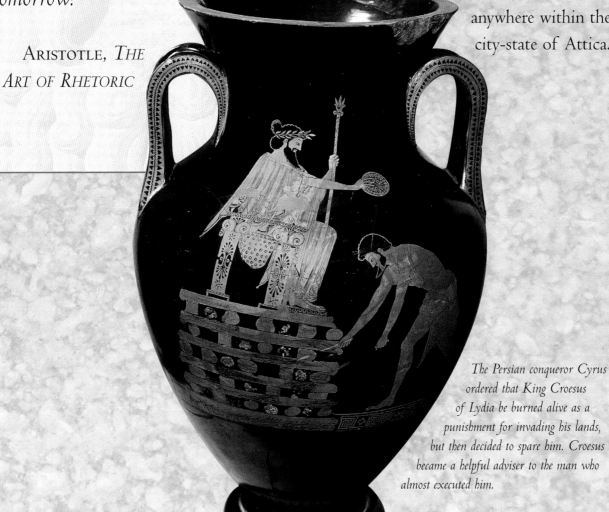

The Persian conqueror Cyrus ordered that King Croesus of Lydia be burned alive as a punishment for invading his lands, but then decided to spare him. Croesus became a helpful adviser to the man who almost executed him.

executed on the plank. The second abducted a slave from our

21

Spartan Law

In the Greek city-state of Sparta, every citizen was a soldier and everything was done to help the city achieve victory in war. Spartan laws were laid down by Lycurgus the lawgiver about 800 B.C. His laws were very strict and were intended to ensure that the Spartans lived simple lives, stayed fit for battle, and were used to obeying orders.

The remains of the agora, or central marketplace, of Sparta. Here, powerful magistrates called ephors condemned criminals to death.

> *Lycurgus would never reduce his laws into writing ... [f]or he thought that the most material points ... being imprinted on the hearts of their youth by a good discipline, would be sure to remain and would find a stronger security, than a compulsion ...*
> PLUTARCH, *LIFE OF LYCURGUS*

compulsion: force

This description of Spartan law explains Lycurgus' idea that laws were best kept by a well-behaved and disciplined people who lived and fought together. To discourage the Spartans from dreaming of wealth, and maybe stealing it from each other, Lycurgus banned them from owning valuables such as gold and silver. Spartan coins were made instead from dull, cheap metals. To prepare the Spartans for the hardships of war, he ordered everyone in the city to eat simple meals together in public kitchens. It was forbidden to hold lavish banquets at home.

... rather than let it be seen.

out his very bowels with its teeth and claws

> So seriously did the ... children go about their stealing, that a youth, having stolen a young fox [to eat] and hid it under his coat, suffered it to tear out his very bowels with its teeth and claws ... rather than let it be seen.
>
> PLUTARCH, *LIFE OF LYCURGUS*

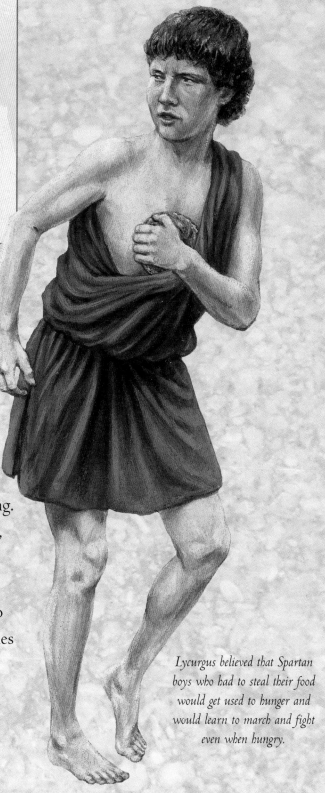

Plutarch explained that Spartan boys were encouraged to steal food. Lycurgus believed that a successful thief needed cunning, patience, and speed. These were also skills that soldiers needed in wartime. Successful boy thieves were praised, and a boy was only flogged if he was caught stealing. In spite of this, Spartan society was civilized, and they passed other laws to encourage discipline and obedience to the law. To show respect to their elders, young Spartans had to keep their hands inside their cloaks at all times and bow their heads if they passed an adult in the street.

Lycurgus believed that Spartan boys who had to steal their food would get used to hunger and would learn to march and fight even when hungry.

Exile

Most exiles were sent out of Athens from the port area of Piraeus. Magistrates patrolled the port to make sure that exiles did not secretly return to the city.

F or the citizens of an ancient Greek city, exile was a terrible punishment. People who were called exiles were cast out from their homeland and forced to leave their family and property behind. They often struggled to make a new life away from their home city and their friends. At best, they would become *metics*, or immigrants with limited legal rights, in another city. The sentence of exile was usually for long periods, such as 10 years or for life.

> [T]he man who is convicted of involuntary homicide shall ... leave the country ... and remain in exile until he is reconciled to one of the relatives of the deceased. Then the law permits him to return ... it instructs him to make sacrifice and to purify himself, and gives other directions for his conduct.
>
> DEMOSTHENES, *AGAINST ARISTOCRATES*

involuntary homicide: killing unintentionally
reconciled to: pardoned by

This law from fifth-century B.C. Athens shows that an exiled killer could only be pardoned by the family of his victim. It also shows that exiles were thought to be unclean until they had gone back to their home city and been purified or cleansed. Exiles were banned from taking part in athletic games such as the Olympics and other religious ceremonies.

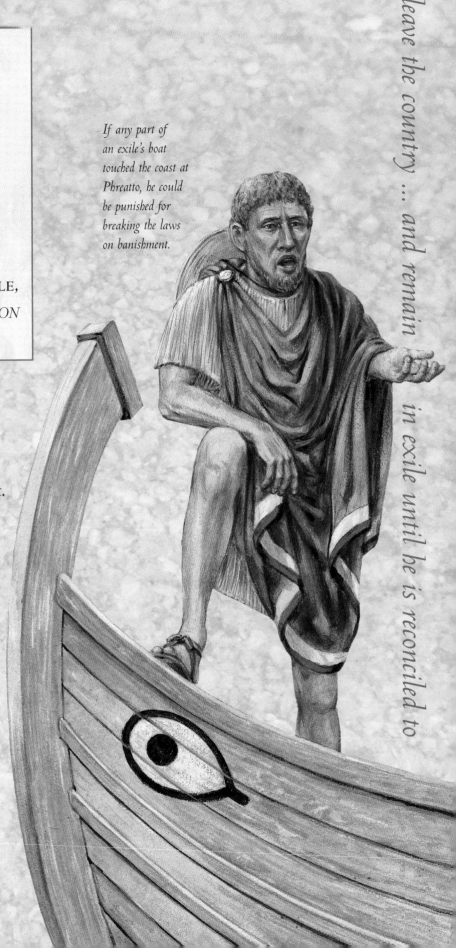

> [W]hen a man has taken refuge in exile after an offense that admits of satisfaction, he is charged with homicide or wounding, he is tried ... and delivers his defense from a ship anchored near the shore.
>
> ARISTOTLE,
> THE ATHENIAN CONSTITUTION

If any part of an exile's boat touched the coast at Phreatto, he could be punished for breaking the laws on banishment.

Greek laws about exile were very strict. Often the property of an exile was confiscated and sold. The houses of exiles were also demolished and the members of their family were treated as outcasts until they had gone through ceremonies of purification. The body of a dead exile couldn't be buried in his homeland without special permission.

Crimes Against the Gods

The ancient Greeks believed that the gods on Mount Olympus, in the far north of Greece, watched over them and noted how they behaved. Someone who offended and angered the gods didn't just bring bad luck on himself but doomed his family, his friends, and his descendants. He also brought shame and ill fortune upon his city.

> [I]f anyone ... shall steal sacred property, he shall be tried before a court, and if he be convicted, he shall not be buried in Attica, and his property shall be confiscated.
>
> XENOPHON, *HELLENICA*

confiscated: taken away

The Athenian laws against sacrilege, or religious crimes, were very strict. Temples had to be especially protected by laws such as this because they were very rich places, filled with gifts given to the gods and the priests. In wartime, when the Greeks captured an enemy city, they even took care not to offend the gods of their defeated enemy.

Part of the Temple of Hera in the ancient Greek colony of Paestum in Italy still stands. As gifts were given to the gods, temples were storehouses of treasure and became a magnet for thieves.

Stealing from a temple offended the gods and could also bring bad luck on your city.

[T]he man who is dead ... worked ... as a field laborer on our farm in Naxos, and one day in a fit of drunken passion he got in a quarrel with one of our ... servants and slew him ... My father bound him ... and then sent to Athens to ask of a diviner what he should do with him.

PLATO, *EUTHYPHRO*

diviner: religious adviser

This description of the character Euthyphro's memory shows that the ancient Greeks worried a lot about upsetting the gods whenever anything unusual happened. Priests and temple officials gave advice on the complicated religious laws in return for a small fee.

All Greeks dreaded being accused of committing a crime against the gods. Because of his great skill, the sculptor Pheidias was a hero in his native city of Athens. However, even he had to flee from the city in 438 B.C. when he was accused of stealing precious materials from the temple of Athena in Athens.

Crimes Against the State

Ancient Greece was made up of many small states, which were often at war with each other. The governments of these states were always afraid that their enemies would try to bribe their citizens to give away secret information or surrender the city. They also worried that their enemies would encourage rebellions against the state. As a result, Greek cities demanded a high degree of loyalty from their citizens and had strict laws against traitors and rebels.

Each year the Athenians voted to banish unpopular citizens. The names of people they wanted to get rid of were scratched on pieces of pottery called ostraca.

The rest of the men [rebels] ... numbering somewhat more than a thousand, were put to death by the Athenians ... They also pulled down the walls of Mytilene and took possession of the Mytilenaean fleet.

THUCYDIDES,
HISTORY OF THE PELOPONNESIAN WAR

Thucydides was an Athenian general who recorded the harsh punishment handed out to the small town of Mytilene, which rebelled unsuccessfully against Athens in 428 B.C. Several years later Thucydides himself was exiled when he failed in a mission and was suspected of treachery, or betrayal. Another Greek general, Phrynichus, was also accused of betrayal. Although he was already dead, his "guilty" bones were dug up and cast out of Greece.

Mytilenaean fleet.

walls of Mytilene and took possession of the

somewhat more than a thousand, were put to death by

> *Socrates is guilty ... as he does not believe in the Gods whom the city worships, but introduces other strange deities; he is also guilty ... as he corrupts the young.*
> DIOGENES LAERTIUS, *LIVES OF THE PHILOSOPHERS*

deities: gods

In this quote, the historian Diogenes describes the most famous trial in Greek history. The Athenian thinker Socrates was accused of betraying the city's gods and teaching the young men of Athens to question their rulers. Socrates was condemned during a religious holiday when execution was forbidden, so he had to wait many days before his sentence could be carried out. As a well-known man, Socrates was not executed on the wooden board but was allowed to die with dignity. Surrounded by his grieving friends, Socrates drank a cup of poison from a hemlock plant.

After being condemned to death, Socrates had 30 days to prepare himself for his execution.

Timeline

All dates are B.C.

c. 2000	The first Greek settlements are founded in the eastern Mediterranean. People agree to live by common laws.
c. 1500	Kings and nobles issue the first law codes to Greek cities.
c. 800	Lycurgus sets down a code of behavior for the Spartans.
620	Draco writes down the earliest-known law code in Athens.
560	Solon gives Athens new laws that are less harsh than Draco's.
c. 510	Athens becomes a more democratic city-state.
c. 500–c. 400	Most surviving Greek law cases date from this period.
445	The Athenian leader Pericles reforms many of the city's laws.
440	The orator Antiphon demands full revenge for the relatives of murder victims.
438	The sculptor Pheidias is accused of stealing from the goddess Athena.
c. 430	Herodotus describes the laws and customs of the ancient world in his *Histories*.
428	The citizens of Mytilene declare their own laws when they rebel against Athens.
c. 423	The playwright Aristophanes mocks Athenian courts in his play *The Wasps*.
c. 410	The first mention of *apotumpanismos* (execution on a wooden board) in the speeches of Lysias.
399	Socrates is sentenced to death by hemlock poisoning.
384	The legal orator Demosthenes is born.
c. 360	Xenophon compares the laws of Athens and Sparta in his *Hellenica*.
350	Aristotle writes his *Athenian Constitution*, describing the city's laws.
c. 200	The coasts of Greece are plagued by pirate raiders.
146	Greece becomes part of the Roman Empire and loses the power to make its own laws.
30	Most Greek cities are using a mixture of Greek and Roman laws by this date.

Glossary

Difficult words from the quoted material appear beside each quotation panel. This glossary explains words used in the main text.

acquitted	Found innocent in a court case.
bylaw	A local law.
chasm	A deep gap or opening in the ground.
citizen	In ancient Greece, a man with full legal rights and powers.
compensation	A payment of money or goods to someone to make up for his or her loss.
condemned	Found guilty in a law court and ordered to be punished.
convicted	Proven guilty of a charge.
defendant	Someone in a law court accused of a crime.
democracy	A state where people choose their leaders.
exile	Forced removal or banishment of a person from his or her homeland.
feud	A lengthy and bitter struggle between individuals or families.
hemlock	A poisonous plant with spotted leaves.
immigrant	Someone who settles in a foreign country.
juror	A citizen who serves on a jury.
jury	A group of citizens selected to decide law cases.
magistrate	A public official or judge.
mercenaries	Soldiers who fight in any army for pay.
obol	An ancient Greek coin worth approximately $2.50 in today's money.
orator	A skilled public speaker.
pension	Money paid to the elderly and retired.
plaque	A tablet or plate bearing a written message.
purification	Making things or people clean in a public ceremony.
stocks	A wooden device for holding offenders, usually by the wrists or ankles.
verdict	The decision made by a jury in a law case.
voluntary	Acting by choice or by one's own free will.

Further Information

Further Reading

Chisholm, Jane. *The Usborne Internet Linked Encyclopaedia of Ancient Greece*. New York: Usborne Publishing, 2002.

Dell, Pamela. *Socrates: Ancient Greek in Search of Truth*. Minneapolis: Compass Point Books, 2007.

Pearson, Anne. *Ancient Greece*. New York: Dorling Kindersley, 2004.

Roberts, Jennifer T., and Tracy Barrett. *Ancient Greek World*. New York: Oxford University Press, 2004.

Solway, Andrew, and Peter Connolly. *Ancient Greece*. New York: Oxford University Press, 2001.

On the Web

For more information on this topic, use FactHound.
1. Go to *www.facthound.com*
2. Type in this book ID: 0756520843
3. Click on the *Fetch It* button.

FactHound will find the best Web sites for you.

Index